WORSHIP TEAM BUILDER

Guiding Your Team from
Formation** to **Fruitfulness

Gerard Assey

WORSHIP TEAM BUILDER:
Guiding Your Team from Formation to Fruitfulness

By

Gerard Assey

Published by:
Gerard Assey
19/18, Palli Arasan Street
Anna Nagar East
Chennai - 600 102

ISBN: 978-81-989262-7-2

Table of Contents

Introduction: The Call to Build

"But the hour is coming, and now is, when the true worshipers will worship the Father in spirit and truth; for the Father is seeking such to worship Him." —**John 4:23** (NKJV)

Worship is Heaven's Priority

Worship is not a church department. It is the heartbeat of Heaven. From Genesis to Revelation, we see worship at the center of God's interaction with His people. Worship is not music—music is merely one of its many expressions. Worship is spiritual alignment—a response to who God is and what He has done.

In John 4:23–24, Jesus makes a startling declaration: the Father is seeking worshipers. Not preachers, not programs, not performers—but worshipers who worship in spirit and truth. That means when we talk about building worship teams, we're not assembling a band—we're training ministers who carry the presence of God.

A Worship Team is a Ministry Team—Not a Music Band

Many churches mistakenly treat the worship team as a group of musicians or vocalists that fill the gap before the sermon. But in truth, the worship team is a ministry team—just like the intercessory team, the pastoral team, or the evangelism team. The difference is: they minister to the Lord first, and then to the people (Acts 13:2).

Just as the Levites in the Old Testament were set apart to minister before the Lord (1 Chronicles 16:4–6), modern-day worship teams are priestly in nature—their role is to create an environment that honors God's presence and invites the congregation into deeper spiritual connection.

The Worship Leader: A Builder, Not Just a Singer

"For every house is built by someone, but He who built all things is God." —Hebrews 3:4 (NKJV)

The worship leader is more than a lead vocalist or skilled instrumentalist—they are called to build:

- ✓ *Build spiritual atmosphere*
- ✓ *Build relational unity*
- ✓ *Build skill and discipline*
- ✓ *Build a team that can function even when they're not on the platform*

God Himself is described as a builder. Jesus said, *"I will build My church"* (Matthew 16:18). If we are made in the image of God and carry His Spirit, we too are called to build. That means as a worship leader or pastor, you are not just preparing songs—you are constructing a people, forming a culture, and raising up worshipers that will outlast you.

Why Many Worship Teams Struggle

Despite good intentions, many worship teams fail to thrive. The issues are rarely about talent. More often, the breakdown is due to:

- ✓ *Lack of clarity in vision or purpose*
- ✓ *Ego clashes and unresolved conflicts*
- ✓ *No discipleship structure or spiritual formation*
- ✓ *Poor communication and unmet expectations*
- ✓ *Burnout from lack of team rhythm and rest*

Worship ministry is both spiritual and structural. Many teams start with enthusiasm but fade out because they didn't know how to move from forming to flourishing.

The Four Stages of Team Development — A Biblical Lens

This book uses the Forming–Storming–Norming–Performing model developed by Bruce Tuckman (1965) as a practical framework for team development. While the model is secular in origin, its principles are deeply biblical. Scripture consistently shows us how people evolve and grow together in groups and ministries.

Let's take a quick look at how this model maps to the Bible:

Stage	**Definition**	**Biblical Example**
Forming	Team is created. Members are excited but uncertain.	Jesus calling His disciples (Luke 5:1–11)
Storming	Conflicts arise. Power struggles and insecurities surface.	Disciples arguing over who is the greatest (Luke 22:24–27)
Norming	Team begins to agree on values, norms, and roles.	Early Church practicing fellowship and unity (Acts 2:42–47)
Performing	Team functions at a high level of maturity and effectiveness.	Paul's missionary teams functioning in harmony (Acts 13 onwards)

This model gives us language and structure to shepherd our teams through the natural stages of growth.

Spirit-Led Structure

The model alone will not transform a team. Many teams go through the motions of planning, rehearsing, and performing without ever becoming united or Spirit-led. That's because no model can replace the presence of God. However, biblical wisdom calls us to pair structure with Spirit, just as Jesus did.

In Mark 6:40, before feeding the multitude, Jesus had the people sit down in groups. He brought order to the chaos, so that what God wanted to release could be received by everyone.

Likewise, in our worship ministries, we must be intentional about how we build. We must bring structure to our vision, form to our function, and discipleship to our culture—so that the glory of God can rest upon us without confusion or division.

What You'll Learn in This Book

In the chapters ahead, you'll discover:

- ✓ *How to form a team with clarity, calling, and spiritual purpose*
- ✓ *How to navigate conflict and ego with biblical wisdom*
- ✓ *How to establish rhythms, values, and unity within your team*
- ✓ *How to lead a team to spiritual maturity and powerful ministry*
- ✓ *How to multiply leaders and build teams that outlast your season*

Each chapter will include:

- ✓ *Biblical examples*
- ✓ *Scripture-based leadership principles*
- ✓ *Practical tools and templates*
- ✓ *Devotionals and reflection moments*

A Final Word Before We Begin

If God has called you to lead worship, He has also called you to build people. You are not merely organizing a weekly song set—you are preparing ministers of God's presence. Just as Nehemiah rebuilt the walls of Jerusalem with a trowel in one hand and a sword in the other, so must you build with skill and Scripture, with strategy and the Spirit.

"Unless the Lord builds the house, they labor in vain who build it." —Psalm 127:1

Let's begin the journey. Let's build worship teams that don't just perform—but worship, grow, minister, and multiply for the glory of God.

Chapter 1: Forming – Laying the Foundation

Theme: Initiating with Intention and Identity

"Then the Lord answered me and said: 'Write the vision and make it plain on tablets, that he may run who reads it.'" —**Habakkuk 2:2** (NKJV)

Why the Forming Stage is Crucial

Every strong building begins with a strong foundation. The Forming stage in team development is where you set the tone, shape the culture, and lay the groundwork. Most problems in ministry teams can be traced back to this phase being rushed or ignored. If you get this right, you prevent confusion, division, and frustration down the line.

This is where the identity and purpose of the worship team is defined, and the right people are aligned with the right roles. It's less about who sings best and more about who serves best.

1. Define the Purpose and Vision

"Write the vision and make it plain…" —Habakkuk 2:2

You cannot build what you have not defined. A vision gives your team something to rally around. Without it, rehearsals become routine, Sunday services become tasks, and team members drift. Begin by asking:

- ✓ *What is the spiritual purpose of our worship team?*
- ✓ *What kind of culture do we want to create?*
- ✓ *What should people experience when we lead worship?*

Example Vision Statement:
"Our worship team exists to create an atmosphere where people encounter God through Spirit-led, skillfully played music, and unified hearts of service. We are ministers first, musicians second."
Practical Action:
Create a Vision Casting Worksheet. Include:

- ✓ *Mission statement*
- ✓ *Core values (e.g., humility, unity, excellence)*
- ✓ *Desired spiritual atmosphere (e.g., reverence, joy, freedom)*
- ✓ *Scriptures that ground your purpose*

2. Select the Right People – Heart Over Skill
"Man looks at the outward appearance, but the Lord looks at the heart." —1 Samuel 16:7
When Samuel went to anoint the next king, he assumed it would be one of Jesse's strong older sons. But God chose David, the youngest, hidden in the field. Why? Because he had the heart of a worshiper (Psalm 78:70–72).
Skill is important (Psalm 33:3), but character matters more:

- ✓ *Choose servants, not stars*
- ✓ *Choose those with a teachable spirit, not just talent*
- ✓ *Choose those who are submitted to the Lord and the church's leadership*

Jesus didn't choose the most impressive disciples—He chose the willing (Luke 5:1–11). He saw potential and called them into purpose.
Practical Action:
Use a New Member Interview Form to assess:

- ✓ *Salvation testimony*
- ✓ *Heart for worship*

- ✓ *Church involvement*
- ✓ *Musical background (secondary)*
- ✓ *Willingness to serve and submit*

3. Cast Vision and Set Expectations

"Where there is no vision, the people perish…" — Proverbs 29:18 (KJV)

Vision must be more than a statement—it must be repeated, taught, and embodied. People do not drift into alignment. They need clarity.

Set expectations in these areas:

- ✓ *Spiritual disciplines (prayer, devotional life)*
- ✓ *Punctuality and preparation for rehearsals*
- ✓ *Dress code or platform presence*
- ✓ *Relational culture (gossip-free, encouraging, humble)*

If not defined, people will bring their own culture in—and that may not match the team's calling.

Practical Tool:

Introduce a Team Covenant that every member reads and signs. It should cover:

- ✓ *Commitment to spiritual growth*
- ✓ *Serving with humility*
- ✓ *Respecting leadership and each other*
- ✓ *Regular attendance and preparedness*

This acts as a spiritual agreement, not legal control.

4. Clarify Roles – Who Does What

"For as the body is one and has many members... so also is Christ." —1 Corinthians 12:12

Even on a small team, confusion about roles causes friction. Clarify:

- ✓ *Who leads songs?*
- ✓ *Who organizes rehearsals?*
- ✓ *Who coordinates with tech/sound teams?*

- ✓ *Who handles scheduling and communication?*

Make it known that every role matters equally—the person on PowerPoint or drums is just as crucial to the encounter as the lead singer. Create a culture of shared honor.

Biblical Insight: Paul teaches that the eye cannot say to the hand, "I don't need you." In a worship team, the platform must reflect unity and mutual respect.

Practical Tool:

Create a Role & Responsibility Chart for your team:

- ✓ *Worship Leader: Vision keeper, flow manager*
- ✓ *Music Director: Arrangements, transitions*
- ✓ *Vocal Leads: Harmonies, lead responsibility*
- ✓ *Instrumentalists: Song mastery, dynamics*
- ✓ *Admin/Coordinator: Schedules, comms*
- ✓ *Sound/Tech: Mixing, projection*

5. The Leader's Role – Encourager, Vision Caster, Welcomer

In the Forming stage, the leader sets the emotional tone and spiritual direction. You are the:

- ✓ *Encourager – You speak life into those who feel unsure or intimidated.*
- ✓ *Vision Caster – You repeat the "why" often and clearly.*
- ✓ *Welcomer – You model inclusion and hospitality.*

Jesus didn't just say, "Come serve Me." He said, "Come follow Me." (Mark 1:17)

Your leadership sets the thermostat for everything. You're not just forming a team; you're forming a culture.

Biblical Case Study: Jesus Calls the First Worship Team (Luke 5:1–11)

Jesus finds Peter, James, and John—not in the temple, but at their workplace, tired and disappointed. He doesn't just perform a miracle of fish—He calls them to a greater purpose: *"From now on you will fish for people."*

Jesus saw potential where others saw ordinary fishermen.

He called them into a vision greater than themselves.

He invited them into relationship, not just responsibility.

You are doing the same when you form your worship team: calling people into Kingdom purpose.

Practical Tools

1. Team Covenant Template

A document every team member signs to commit to:

- ✓ *Regular devotional life*
- ✓ *Unity and humility*
- ✓ *Submission to leadership*
- ✓ *Excellence in preparation*
- ✓ *Being a role model on and off the platform*

(Add space for signatures and date.)

2. Vision Casting Worksheet

Includes:

- ✓ *Mission statement*
- ✓ *Core values (e.g., reverence, joy, growth, service)*
- ✓ *Scriptures that reflect team identity (e.g., John 4:23–24, Psalm 133)*
- ✓ *Short- and long-term goals*
- ✓ *Opportunities for feedback and buy-in from the team*

3. New Member Onboarding Checklist

☐ Interview with Worship Leader
☐ Attend 2 rehearsals as observer
☐ Read & sign team covenant
☐ Provide availability and schedule commitment
☐ Assigned to a mentor or buddy
☐ Added to team communication channels

Final Encouragement

In the Forming stage, you are not just gathering musicians—you are assembling a priesthood. Take your time. Lay the foundation deep. Pray over every member. Instruct with the Word. Build with wisdom. Don't settle for mere sound—build for substance.

"Through wisdom a house is built, and by understanding it is established." —Proverbs 24:3

When you begin with intention and identity, the rest of the journey becomes fruitful.

Chapter 2:
Storming – Facing Friction with Faith

Theme: Navigating Conflict, Clashes, and Insecurities
"My brethren, count it all joy when you fall into various trials, knowing that the testing of your faith produces patience." —**James 1:2–3** (NKJV)

Welcome to the Storming Stage
Every team—no matter how anointed, talented, or prayerful—will go through conflict. In fact, conflict is part of growth. The "Storming" stage in team development is where tension rises, personalities clash, and insecurities surface. If handled well, these storms can lead to maturity, depth, and trust. If ignored, they can lead to breakdown and division.
Think of this stage as a refiner's fire. It's painful but purifying. God uses this stage to expose motives, surface hidden wounds, and develop spiritual muscles in your team.

1. Why This Stage is Necessary for Growth
"...the testing of your faith produces patience." — James 1:3
In the early days of forming a team, everyone is on their best behavior. But over time, real personalities show up:

- ✓ *The perfectionist who gets frustrated with others*
- ✓ *The quiet one who feels overlooked*
- ✓ *The talented singer who wants more solos*
- ✓ *The faithful but less skilled member who feels left behind*

These tensions are not signs of failure. They're signs of formation. God is shaping hearts, not just harmonies.

Biblical Insight:

Even the disciples fought among themselves. In Luke 22:24, they argued about who among them was the greatest—*during the Last Supper!* Jesus didn't dismiss them. He used it as a teaching moment to call them to servanthood.

2. Common Worship Team Tensions

Understanding where conflict commonly arises will help you stay proactive. Here are the most frequent friction points:

Egos and Recognition

- ✓ *"Why didn't I get to lead the main song?"*
- ✓ *"They always choose her and not me."*

Biblical Root: Pride and insecurity.

Solution: Teach identity in Christ, not platform performance.

Musical Styles and Preferences

- ✓ *"I prefer contemporary worship."*
- ✓ *"We should sing more hymns."*

Biblical Root: Personal preference over corporate purpose.

Solution: Define vision clearly—worship is about glorifying God, not style wars (Colossians 3:16–17).

Theological Differences

- ✓ *"Should we sing songs from that church?"*
- ✓ *"What about songs that repeat too much?"*

Biblical Root: Differences in doctrine or discernment.

Solution: Anchor song choices in Scripture and church leadership, not trends.

Time Commitment & Priorities

- ✓ *"I'm busy this week—can I skip practice?"*
- ✓ *"Do I really need to be there early?"*

Biblical Root: Misunderstanding ministry as service vs. convenience.
Solution: Remind the team of sacrificial service (Romans 12:1).

3. Healthy Confrontation – The Biblical Way

"If your brother sins against you, go and tell him his fault between you and him alone..." —Matthew 18:15
Jesus gave us a clear, simple, and powerful model for resolving conflict. Sadly, it's often ignored.
The Matthew 18 Model:

- ✓ *Go privately – Not on WhatsApp. Not in rehearsal. One-on-one.*
- ✓ *Speak with grace and truth – Not accusations. Speak to build.*
- ✓ *If unresolved, bring one or two others – A neutral leader, not your backup singers.*
- ✓ *Escalate only when necessary – Involve pastoral leadership when restoration is impossible without oversight.*

Key Principle: Confrontation is not about being right. It's about being reconciled.
"Blessed are the peacemakers…" (Matthew 5:9)

4. Building Unity Through Communication

"Walk worthy... with all lowliness and gentleness, with longsuffering, bearing with one another in love..." —Ephesians 4:1–3

Miscommunication is one of the fastest ways to divide a team. Misunderstood messages, overlooked feelings, or sarcasm can poison the atmosphere. Unity isn't automatic—it must be cultivated.

Practical Practices for Unity:

- ✓ *Start rehearsals with a 5-minute check-in or prayer circle*
- ✓ *Use "I" language in feedback (e.g., "I felt confused when…")*
- ✓ *Encourage open-door conversations*
- ✓ *Make space for people to voice discomfort without fear*

5. Leader's Role: Mediator, Truth Teller, Anchor in Love

During the storming phase, you must step into a pastoral leadership role, not just a musical director. You are:

- ✓ Mediator – Helping people listen and be heard
- ✓ Truth Teller – Speaking correction in love (Ephesians 4:15)
- ✓ Anchor in Love – Remaining calm and Spirit-led even in heated moments

"A soft answer turns away wrath…" —Proverbs 15:1

"Open rebuke is better than hidden love…" —Proverbs 27:5

Your tone, posture, and spiritual maturity will set the standard for the team. People will take cues from how you respond to conflict.

Biblical Case Study: Paul and Barnabas (Acts 15:36–41)

Paul and Barnabas were anointed apostles and close friends. Yet they had a sharp disagreement over John Mark's involvement on their next missionary trip. So sharp, in fact, that they parted ways.

Lessons from this conflict:

- ✓ *Even godly people can disagree strongly*
- ✓ *Conflict doesn't disqualify you—it reveals your heart*
- ✓ *Sometimes separation is needed for growth (both teams went on to minister fruitfully)*

Years later, Paul commends John Mark again (2 Timothy 4:11), showing that reconciliation is possible over time.

Practical Tools

1. **Conflict Resolution Guide (Matthew 18 Based)**

Step	Action	Scripture
1	Talk privately, one-on-one	Matthew 18:15
2	Bring 1–2 mature believers	Matthew 18:16
3	Involve leadership	Matthew 18:17
4	Choose forgiveness and reconciliation	Colossians 3:13
5	Move forward in peace	Romans 12:18

2. Unity-Building Devotionals (Sample Topics)

You can use these for weekly devotionals or personal team reflection.

- ✓ "One Body, Many Parts" – 1 Corinthians 12
- ✓ "Let Love Lead" – 1 Peter 4:8
- ✓ "Pleasing God, Not People" – Galatians 1:10
- ✓ "Guarding the Heart" – Proverbs 4:23
- ✓ "Love Does Not Envy" – 1 Corinthians 13:4–7

3. Listening & Empathy Exercises

During team time or retreat:

- ✓ The "Two-Minute Rule": One member shares something personal. Everyone else listens without interrupting. Builds empathy and trust.
- ✓ Affirmation Circle: Every member affirms something positive about the person next to them.
- ✓ Role Reversal: Singers and musicians exchange mock roles and explain their challenges to build mutual appreciation.

Final Encouragement

Conflict is uncomfortable, but it is not unholy. God often uses the storming stage to teach us humility, empathy, forgiveness, and spiritual maturity. Don't fear the friction—face it with faith.

"Iron sharpens iron…" —Proverbs 27:17

"Be kindly affectionate to one another... in honor giving preference to one another." —Romans 12:10

As you lovingly lead your team through this season, you are not just managing personalities—you are discipling hearts and building character. On the other side of this storm is something beautiful: a unified, mature, Spirit-filled worship team that truly ministers in harmony.

Chapter 3:
Norming – Creating Culture and Chemistry

Theme: Establishing Rhythms, Roles, and Relationship
"Fulfill my joy by being like-minded, having the same love, being of one accord, of one mind." — **Philippians 2:2** (NKJV)

The Norming Stage: From Individual to Team
After surviving the storm, the team begins to settle into shared understanding and mutual respect. This is the Norming stage—where alignment takes root, relationships deepen, and the team begins functioning as a unified body.
But make no mistake—unity doesn't happen automatically. It must be cultivated through intentional rhythms, clear roles, and a strong relational culture. Without these, the team may regress into conflict or fall into complacency.

1. Agreement on Values, Culture, and Practice
"Let nothing be done through selfish ambition or conceit, but in lowliness of mind let each esteem others better than himself..." —Philippians 2:3
The best teams aren't built on talent alone—they are built on shared values. When every team member knows "how we do things here," the culture becomes self-sustaining. That's when trust and chemistry develop.

Three Areas of Agreement:
Spiritual values– Worship is ministry, not performance
– We serve with humility and joy
– We prioritize prayer and unity
Relational values
– We honor each other
– We speak truth in love
– We forgive quickly
Practical values
– We are punctual
– We prepare for rehearsals
– We submit to leadership
"Can two walk together, unless they are agreed?" — Amos 3:3
Agreement builds momentum. Disagreement breeds confusion.

2. Developing Team Devotion Habits
One of the greatest tragedies in many worship teams is that they sound great but are spiritually dry. In the Norming stage, it's essential to introduce consistent devotional practices—not just for the group, but also individually.
Why Team Devotion Matters:
- ✓ *Keeps the heart of worship alive*
- ✓ *Protects the team from pride and burnout*
- ✓ *Builds spiritual intimacy and trust*

Devotion Formats You Can Use:
- ✓ Short Word + Worship + Prayer before every rehearsal
- ✓ Weekly team devotional on WhatsApp or email
- ✓ Monthly "Worship Nights" focused purely on prayer and ministry

Assign each team member to lead a devotional in rotation

Biblical Insight:

The early church "devoted themselves to the apostles' teaching and to fellowship, to the breaking of bread and to prayer" (Acts 2:42). Devotion must come before direction.

3. Commitment to Excellence and Growth

"And whatever you do, do it heartily, as to the Lord and not to men..." —Colossians 3:23

Excellence is not about being perfect—it's about giving God our very best. When a team values growth over comfort, it naturally moves forward.

Characteristics of Excellence-Oriented Teams:

- ✓ Practice regularly, not just before Sundays
- ✓ Welcome feedback without offense
- ✓ Help one another improve without competition
- ✓ Take personal ownership of preparation

Old Testament Example: The craftsmen who built the Tabernacle were "skilled, gifted by the Spirit, and willing-hearted" (Exodus 31:1–6). God honors excellence that flows from a consecrated heart.

Leader's Role Here:

- ✓ Set clear expectations for practice and preparation
- ✓ Celebrate growth, not just results
- ✓ Offer specific, kind, and actionable feedback
- ✓ Provide opportunities for training and upskilling

4. Leader's Role: Culture Shaper, Model, Coach

During this stage, your influence as a leader is foundational. You are:

- ✓ The Culture Shaper – You define and reinforce the team's values and spiritual DNA.
- ✓ The Model – You exemplify humility, punctuality, preparation, and prayer.
- ✓ The Coach – You guide team members to grow in skill, character, and confidence.

"Imitate me, just as I also imitate Christ." —1 Corinthians 11:1

Coaching Questions to Ask Regularly:

- ✓ *How are you doing spiritually?*
- ✓ *What are you practicing musically?*
- ✓ *How do you feel you're growing as a worshiper?*
- ✓ *What do you need from me as a leader?*

The goal is to raise up a team that functions with or without you—a self-led culture under the Lordship of Christ.

Biblical Case Study: Nehemiah – Building With Clarity and Cooperation (Nehemiah 3)

Nehemiah didn't just pray—he organized people. In Nehemiah 3, we see:

- ✓ People assigned to specific portions of the wall
- ✓ Families and clans working side by side
- ✓ Each person knowing their role and responsibility
- ✓ A clear structure, yet a shared spirit of purpose

This is the picture of healthy Norming. Worship teams must likewise be:

- ✓ *Organized but relational*
- ✓ *Role-driven but united in purpose*
- ✓ *Gifted but humble*

When everyone plays their part, God's glory is built in the midst of the people.

Practical Tools

1. Weekly Worship Team Meeting Format

Suggested Agenda (45–60 min weekly):

- ✓ Opening Prayer & Short Devotional (10 min)
- ✓ Check-in Round: "How are you?" (5–10 min)
- ✓ Upcoming Schedule & Planning (5 min)
- ✓ Practice & Song Review (30–40 min)
- ✓ Final Thoughts & Prayer Circle (5 min)

Pro Tip: End every meeting with an "encouragement moment" – let each member speak a word of thanks or affirmation to another.

2. Sample Devotional Outlines for Worship Teams

Devotional 1: "Worship is a Lifestyle"
Text: Romans 12:1
Focus: Worship extends beyond the stage
Question: *How do I worship God in my daily life?*

Devotional 2: "Serving with Joy"
Text: Psalm 100:2
Focus: Attitude matters more than applause
Question: *Am I joyfully serving or quietly complaining?*

Devotional 3: "Guarding the Heart"
Text: Proverbs 4:23
Focus: Dealing with jealousy, comparison, and pride
Question: *Is my heart aligned with God's?*

3. Skill-Sharing & Buddy Mentorship System

This system pairs newer or developing members with experienced ones to foster both skill and relationship.

Buddy Responsibilities:

- ✓ *Pray with and for each other weekly*
- ✓ *Review one song together before Sunday*
- ✓ *Share spiritual insights from personal devotion*
- ✓ *Encourage each other after every service*

Bonus: Have quarterly "Buddy Swap" to build wider team relationships.

Final Encouragement

When your team enters the Norming phase, you have a golden opportunity: to shape not just a sound, but a spirit. This is where a group becomes a family, and a band becomes a body.

"Let us not grow weary while doing good..." — Galatians 6:9

Lay strong rhythms. Clarify roles. Build relationships. As you do, God will knit your team together with cords that no conflict can sever.

You are now building a worship culture that Heaven can trust.

Chapter 4:
Performing – Leading with Purpose and Power

Theme: Ministering as One, in Spirit and Truth
"Behold, how good and how pleasant it is for brethren to dwell together in unity... for there the Lord commanded the blessing—life forevermore." — **Psalm 133:1, 3** (NKJV)

The Performing Stage: From Team to Ministry Force
In the Performing stage, the worship team moves from functioning to flourishing. The group is no longer a collection of individuals—they have become one body, one spirit, one voice.
This stage is not about performance in the worldly sense. It's about ministering with maturity, unity, and spiritual authority. The team flows seamlessly together, not because of perfect rehearsals alone, but because of deep alignment of heart, mission, and Spirit.

1. Becoming a Spiritually Mature, United, and Effective Team
At this stage:
- ✓ Team members take personal responsibility for spiritual preparation.
- ✓ Conflict is handled with maturity, not drama.
- ✓ People look for ways to serve, not shine.
- ✓ The group moves from managing ministry to multiplying it.

"Therefore, leaving the discussion of the elementary principles of Christ, let us go on to perfection..." — Hebrews 6:1

Indicators of Maturity:

- ✓ Team members pray together spontaneously
- ✓ Members cover each other in grace, not gossip
- ✓ There is joyful submission to leadership and to one another
- ✓ The team ministers with spiritual sensitivity, not mechanical routine

Biblical Example:

David and his appointed Levites (1 Chronicles 25) weren't just skillful musicians; they were trained, anointed, and spiritually mature men who prophesied on their instruments. They flowed in both excellence and spiritual insight.

2. Flowing Together Under the Anointing

"...it is like the precious oil upon the head... running down on the beard... running down on the edge of his garments." —Psalm 133:2

Unity is not just organizational—it's spiritual. When a worship team is united in heart and purpose, the anointing flows from the top (leadership) to every part of the team and out into the congregation.

This is where worship becomes transformational, not just inspirational. It's where the atmosphere shifts, chains break, and people encounter the presence of God—not because the music is flawless, but because the hearts are yielded.

How to Cultivate Flow:

- ✓ Stay submitted to the Holy Spirit, even during services

- ✓ Be flexible to follow spontaneous promptings (e.g., repeating a bridge, changing a song)
- ✓ Practice the "eye and ear" connection—reading the leader's visual and spiritual cues
- ✓ Maintain strong spiritual and emotional health behind the scenes

3. Empowering Others and Sharing Leadership

"And the things that you have heard from me... commit these to faithful men who will be able to teach others also." —2 Timothy 2:2

A sign of a high-performing worship team is that leadership is distributed. One person may carry the vision, but everyone carries responsibility.

What Shared Leadership Looks Like:

- ✓ Different people leading worship sets
- ✓ Musicians rotating leadership of rehearsals
- ✓ Vocalists mentoring newer singers
- ✓ Team members taking initiative in planning or outreach

Biblical Example:

In Acts 6, when the apostles became overwhelmed, they delegated leadership to trustworthy men, empowering them to serve the body. This enabled greater effectiveness and multiplication.

When worship leaders empower their teams, the result is ownership, energy, and legacy.

4. Leader's Role: Equipper, Empowerer, Encourager

At this stage, the leader must shift from "doer" to "developer."

You are no longer needed to manage every detail. Your calling is to:

- ✓ Equip – Teach people how to minister, not just perform
- ✓ Empower – Release them to lead without micromanaging
- ✓ Encourage – Speak life constantly, especially after ministry moments

"He gave some to be... pastors and teachers, to equip the saints for the work of ministry..." — Ephesians 4:11–12

As the leader, your quiet presence and strong foundation become the platform for others to shine for God's glory.

Biblical Case Study: The Early Church Worship Gatherings (Acts 2:42–47)

"They continued steadfastly in the apostles' doctrine and fellowship, in the breaking of bread, and in prayers..."

In this passage, we find the ideal model of a performing team:

- ✓ Unity in doctrine and practice
- ✓ Devotion to spiritual rhythms
- ✓ Generosity and selflessness
- ✓ Growth in number and impact

They were not a "worship team" as we define it today, but they had a deep culture of worship. They weren't focused on stage presence but on God's presence—and it produced supernatural results.

The same can happen when worship teams lead with purpose, power, and unity.

Practical Tools

1. Sunday Preparation Checklist

Spiritual Prep:

☐ Prayed over the set list

☐ Read and meditated on relevant Scriptures
☐ Checked in with team spiritually/emotionally
Technical Prep:
☐ Reviewed chord charts and arrangements
☐ Rehearsed transitions and dynamics
☐ Coordinated with sound/media team
Relational Prep:
☐ Encouraged team members before service
☐ Prayed together as a team
☐ Maintained joy and peace throughout rehearsal

2. Evaluation and Feedback Template

Use weekly or monthly for personal and group reflection.

Area	**Reflection Questions**	**Notes**
Spiritual Flow	Did we stay sensitive to the Spirit?	
Team Unity	Were we in sync, encouraging each other?	
Musical Execution	Were transitions smooth and prepared?	
Congregational Engagement	Did we invite people into worship or entertain?	
Personal Growth	What did I learn this week?	

3. Leadership Development Plan for Team Members

Develop future leaders from within your team.

Step-by-Step Plan:

- ✓ Identify potential – Look for humility, faithfulness, and initiative
- ✓ Assign responsibilities – Let them plan a set or run a rehearsal
- ✓ Mentor regularly – Meet monthly for spiritual and leadership growth
- ✓ Expose to higher levels – Include them in planning meetings, retreats
- ✓ Release slowly – Give increasing levels of responsibility and feedback
- ✓ Biblical Model: Jesus trained His disciples over time, gave them tasks (Luke 9), corrected them in love, and eventually released them (Matthew 28:19–20).

Final Encouragement

The Performing stage is a reward for endurance and obedience. This is where you will witness:

- ✓ People encountering God deeply
- ✓ Team members walking in freedom and purpose
- ✓ The anointing flowing with power
- ✓ New leaders rising and taking the vision further

But remember: this stage is not the end—it's a platform. A true worship team doesn't peak at performance—it reproduces legacy.

"Those who are planted in the house of the Lord shall flourish..." —Psalm 92:13

So lead with purpose. Minister with power. Serve with humility. And may your worship team become a channel of God's glory every time they take the platform.

Chapter 5:
Beyond Performing – Multiplying the Mission

Theme: Reproducing Healthy Teams & Leaving Legacy
"And the things that you have heard from me among many witnesses, commit these to faithful men who will be able to teach others also." —**2 Timothy 2:2** (NKJV)

From Fruitfulness to Faithful Multiplication

Once a worship team reaches the Performing stage, many leaders make the mistake of stopping there. The team is doing well. The services are powerful. People are blessed. But if you stop here, you risk falling into stagnation or burnout.

God's heart is not just that you lead worship effectively, but that you raise up others to lead and reproduce healthy teams that carry the vision forward. This chapter focuses on legacy, multiplication, and long-term sustainability.

1. The Cycle of Multiplying Leaders and Teams

"Commit these to faithful men who will be able to teach others also." —2 Timothy 2:2

Paul's instruction to Timothy is a blueprint for generational discipleship:

- ✓ Teach others.
- ✓ Equip them to teach others in turn.
- ✓ Create a chain of faith and fruitfulness.

In the context of worship teams, this means:

- ✓ Training new leaders

- ✓ Mentoring younger or newer members
- ✓ Preparing the team to outgrow your own leadership

Multiplication is not about losing control—it's about expanding influence.

Biblical Example:

Jesus didn't just lead worship moments—He discipled future leaders. The result? Worship spread from the Upper Room to the ends of the earth (Acts 1–2).

2. Avoiding Burnout Through Delegation and Rest

"The thing that you do is not good... You will surely wear yourself out, both you and these people with you." —Exodus 18:17–18

Moses was trying to do it all—judge, lead, counsel, and guide—until Jethro wisely advised him to delegate responsibility. Leaders who fail to delegate in worship ministry often end up:

- ✓ Burning out
- ✓ Frustrating their team
- ✓ Stunting team growth

Your job is not to be the main act every Sunday, but to build a sustainable structure where others can flourish.

"Come to Me... I will give you rest." —Matthew 11:28

Rest is a command, not a suggestion.

Delegate the Right Way:

- ✓ Delegate with clarity (don't make people guess what you want)
- ✓ Delegate with authority (let them make real decisions)
- ✓ Delegate with accountability (give feedback, not criticism)

Biblical Example:
Elijah thought he was the only one left (1 Kings 19:10), but God revealed that there were 7,000 others. Soon after, Elijah began to mentor Elisha, raising up a prophetic successor.

3. Establishing a Worship Discipleship Pipeline
If you want to leave a legacy, you must build a system—not just rely on personality. This is where a Worship Discipleship Pipeline becomes essential.
Discipleship Pipeline Stages:
Observer Stage
- ✓ New person watches, listens, and attends rehearsals
- ✓ Introduced to team culture and values

Apprentice Stage
- ✓ Begins helping in small ways (e.g., harmonies, tech, devotionals)
- ✓ Receives one-on-one mentoring

Contributor Stage
- ✓ Takes on full participation in ministry
- ✓ Leads sections of worship or practice
- ✓ Starts mentoring someone else

Leader Stage
- ✓ Oversees part of the ministry (e.g., band, vocals, logistics)
- ✓ Plans sets, leads teams, teaches others

Biblical Examples:
Moses raised up Joshua (Exodus 33:11) who eventually led Israel into the Promised Land
Elijah trained Elisha, who received a double portion and continued the ministry (2 Kings 2:9–15)
This is the pattern of biblical leadership: relationship, impartation, and release.

Leader's Role: Legacy-Builder, System-Creator, Kingdom-Multiplier

You are no longer just a worship leader—you are now a legacy builder.

Your focus must now shift to:

- ✓ Building systems that outlive you
- ✓ Developing leaders who can take the vision further
- ✓ Encouraging spiritual growth, not just musical skill

"One plants, another waters, but God gives the increase." —1 Corinthians 3:6

Biblical Case Study: Moses and Joshua | Elijah and Elisha

Moses → Joshua

Moses took Joshua everywhere:

- ✓ Up the mountain (Exodus 24:13)
- ✓ Into the Tent of Meeting (Exodus 33:11)
- ✓ On the battlefield (Exodus 17:10)

Joshua wasn't the loudest, most visible, or most talented—but he was faithful, and he absorbed Moses' heart. Eventually, he led Israel into victory.

Elijah → Elisha

Elisha followed Elijah closely, refusing to be left behind (2 Kings 2). His legacy? A double portion and a ministry that exceeded Elijah's reach.

This is what happens when we pour into others intentionally: the work of God multiplies.

Practical Tools

1. Worship Intern/Apprentice Pathway Plan

Stage	**Activities**	**Goals**
Observer	Attend rehearsals, shadow team	Learn culture, expectations
Apprentice	Serve in minor roles (backup vocals, tech support)	Develop commitment, character
Junior Leader	Co-lead songs, plan sets	Grow skill, spiritual maturity
Team Leader	Lead full sets, mentor others	Multiply and sustain vision

Mentor Check-ins: Bi-weekly for guidance, prayer, and growth tracking.

2. Team Succession Plan Template

Area	**Current Leader**	**Apprentice**	**Timeline for Transition**
Worship Leader	[Name]	[Name]	[3–6 months]
Band Leader	[Name]	[Name]	[6 months]
Vocal Leader	[Name]	[Name]	[6 months]
Tech Team Head	[Name]	[Name]	[3 months]

Succession ensures continuity without crisis.

3. Ministry Calendar Template

Plan for long-term rhythm, not just weekly services.

Month	Activity	Purpose
Jan	Worship Retreat	Refocus and realign vision
Mar	Skill Workshop	Grow practical ability
Jun	Worship Night	Minister to church/community
Aug	Mid-Year Evaluation	Assess health and goals
Oct	Guest Training/Equipping	Fresh input from other leaders
Dec	Appreciation Dinner	Celebrate, honour, refresh

Keep the calendar balanced between input (growth) and output (ministry).

Final Encouragement

You were never meant to do ministry alone. The ultimate mark of your leadership is not how well you lead worship—it's how well you raise others to lead worship after you.

"Even to the next generation, Your praises will be declared." —Psalm 145:4 (Paraphrased)

As you build a culture of discipleship, multiplication, and intentional rest, you are not just maintaining a team—you're building the future of worship in your church.

Let your ceiling become someone else's floor.

Let your voice echo in the next generation.

Let the mission multiply.

Conclusion:
From Stage to Sanctuary

Theme: The Worship Leader as Shepherd and Steward
"And He is the head of the body, the church… that in all things He may have the preeminence." —**Colossians 1:18** (NKJV)

The Journey So Far
You've walked through the full life cycle of building a worship team—from Forming, Storming, Norming, Performing, and beyond. These aren't just leadership stages—they are discipleship journeys that mirror the spiritual maturing of a people entrusted with a holy calling.
But now we step into something deeper: understanding the worship leader not as just a director of music, but as a shepherd of people and a steward of sacred trust.

1. The Worship Leader as Shepherd
Worship leading is pastoral leadership, not a performance-based role. You may not carry the title of "Pastor," but in function, you are:

- ✓ Shepherding hearts
- ✓ Guiding people into the presence of God
- ✓ Protecting unity
- ✓ Feeding the team with truth
- ✓ Leading by example in holiness and humility

Biblical Examples:
David – Before he was king, he was a shepherd-musician. He played his harp to calm Saul (1 Samuel 16:23), protected sheep with his life (1 Samuel

17:34–35), and wrote psalms of worship. His leadership flowed from intimacy with God and care for others.

Jesus – The Good Shepherd (John 10:11) laid down His life for the sheep. He knew them by name, went after the lost, and led with tenderness and truth.

"Shepherd the flock of God which is among you… being examples to the flock." —1 Peter 5:2–3

You don't just lead songs—you lead souls.

2. The Worship Leader as Steward

A steward is someone who manages what belongs to someone else. As a worship leader, you don't own the platform, the people, or even your gift. All of it belongs to God.

"Moreover it is required in stewards that one be found faithful." —1 Corinthians 4:2

What are you stewarding?

- ✓ **Time** – Are rehearsals meaningful and purposeful?
- ✓ **Talent** – Are you developing and deploying people's gifts for God's glory?
- ✓ **Team** – Are you cultivating spiritual health, not just musical excellence?
- ✓ **Truth** – Are your song choices biblically sound and theologically rich?
- ✓ **Tone** – Are you setting a Christ-centered culture of honor, humility, and joy?

Stewardship is the secret to long-term fruitfulness.

3. Keeping Christ at the Center

It's easy to get caught up in:

- ✓ Weekly song planning
- ✓ Technical excellence
- ✓ Rotas and rehearsals

- ✓ Lighting, sound, and slides

But the danger is we may unintentionally shift from worshipping God to worshipping the work of God.

"That in all things He may have the preeminence." —Colossians 1:18

Practical Ways to Keep Christ Central:

- ✓ Begin every rehearsal with Scripture and prayer—real prayer, not just a "Lord, bless this time."
- ✓ Remind the team regularly: "We are here to serve, not to be seen."
- ✓ Teach the team to minister even if there's no music—because worship is heart posture, not stage setup.
- ✓ Occasionally strip it all down—no slides, no lights, just voices before God.

Jesus must remain the center of our worship—not the song set, not the skill, not the stage.

4. Final Encouragement: The Invisible Impact

Worship leadership may not always get applause, visibility, or recognition. But in heaven's eyes, it is deeply precious. Every time you:

- ✓ Pray for a team member behind the scenes
- ✓ Say no to a solo so someone else can grow
- ✓ Show up early to help set up
- ✓ Encourage instead of criticize
- ✓ Point hearts to Christ in quiet faithfulness—

You are building an eternal altar of worship.

"For God is not unjust to forget your work and labor of love..." —Hebrews 6:10

The sanctuary you are building is not made of lights and instruments—it is made of lives. Lives that are drawn into intimacy with Jesus because of your obedience, humility, and leadership.

Prayer of Commissioning

Let's end this journey by praying a prayer of commissioning over your life and leadership.

Father,
Thank You for the privilege of leading worship—not as a task, but as a calling.
Thank You for entrusting me with a team to shepherd, a platform to steward, and a people to serve.
Help me keep Jesus at the center of every rehearsal, every set list, every decision, and every conversation.
Let my leadership be marked not by talent, but by truth, not by charisma, but by character.
Make me a builder of people, not platforms. A releaser of gifts, not a keeper of control.
Help me steward hearts, not just harmonies.
Raise up others around me. Let the next generation go further, fly higher, and burn brighter.
And let every song we sing echo not only in sanctuaries, but in the chambers of heaven.
I commit this worship ministry to You, Lord.
It is for You, through You, and unto You.
In Jesus' mighty name,
Amen.

Your Next Step: Keep Building

Your team will shift between stages at different times. New members will come. Seasons will change. Conflicts may arise again. But now you are equipped to shepherd your team through every phase, with the Word as your foundation and the Spirit as your guide.
Keep building. Keep discipling. Keep multiplying.
And above all… keep worshipping.

Leader's Toolkit: A Practical Guide for Worship Team Builders

"Let every skillful craftsman among you come and make all that the Lord has commanded." —**Exodus 35:10** (ESV)

This toolkit is designed to help Worship Leaders, Pastors, and Ministry Builders lead their teams with wisdom, structure, and grace. Use it during planning, mentoring, training, and evaluation across all five team-building stages.

---

1. Team Covenant Template

"Can two walk together, unless they are agreed?" —Amos 3:3

Use this to set expectations at the Forming stage.

Worship Team Covenant

We, as members of the Worship Ministry, commit to:

- ✓ *Serve with humility, excellence, and joy (Philippians 2:3; Colossians 3:23)*
- ✓ *Be punctual, prepared, and prayerful*
- ✓ *Submit to leadership and each other (Ephesians 5:21)*
- ✓ *Honor our personal time with God before platform time*
- ✓ *Speak truth in love and pursue unity (Ephesians 4:15–16)*
- ✓ *Grow in our gifts and help others grow in theirs*

Signed by:
Team Member: ______________________ Date: ___________

Worship Leader: ______________________ Date: ___________

---

2. Vision Casting Worksheet

"Write the vision and make it plain on tablets..." — Habakkuk 2:2

Use this to help articulate purpose in a team meeting or retreat.

WORSHIP MINISTRY VISION WORKSHEET

- ✓ What is our primary purpose as a team?
- ✓ What kind of culture do we want to build?
- ✓ What do we want people to experience when we lead worship?
- ✓ How do we measure success?
- ✓ What Scriptures define our identity as a worship team?

(Suggested Scriptures: John 4:23–24, Romans 12:1, Psalm 100:2, 1 Peter 2:9)

---

3. New Member Onboarding Checklist

"Let all things be done decently and in order." —1 Corinthians 14:40

Ensure every new member transitions smoothly.

Task	Completed?
Attended worship team orientation session	☐
Read and signed Team Covenant	☐
Introduced to team mentor/buddy	☐

Task	Completed?
Given access to setlist platform/group chat	☐
Received weekly rehearsal schedule	☐
Participated in first devotional	☐
Joined worship planning meeting as observer	☐

---

4. Conflict Resolution Model (Matthew 18 Template)

"If your brother sins against you, go and tell him his fault between you and him alone." —Matthew 18:15

Step 1: Private Conversation

Speak to the person directly, in love.

Step 2: Bring a Witness (leader/mentor)

If unresolved, bring a neutral team leader.

Step 3: Leadership Involvement

If still unresolved, escalate to the pastor or elder overseeing worship.

Step 4: Restoration or Release

Choose grace-filled outcomes. Always aim for healing and unity.

Tip: Always address tension before it festers. Unity must be protected proactively.

---

5. Weekly Worship Team Meeting Format

"They continued steadfastly in the apostles' doctrine and fellowship..." —Acts 2:42

Suggested Flow (60–75 minutes):

- ✓ Welcome & Icebreaker (5 min)
- ✓ Devotional & Prayer (10–15 min)

- ✓ Check-in Round (How's everyone doing?) (10 min)
- ✓ Worship Set Planning / Feedback (10–15 min)
- ✓ Skill Training / Team Development (10–20 min)
- ✓ Rehearsal & Song Practice (15–30 min)
- ✓ Wrap-up & Encouragement Circle (5 min)

---

6. Spiritual Health Check-In Questions

"Examine yourselves as to whether you are in the faith..." —2 Corinthians 13:5

Use monthly in mentoring or one-on-one settings.

- ✓ *How is your personal walk with God this month?*
- ✓ *What has God been teaching you lately?*
- ✓ *Are you finding joy in worship ministry?*
- ✓ *How are you managing spiritual, emotional, and physical fatigue?*
- ✓ *Is there any relationship tension you need help resolving?*
- ✓ *How can I pray for you?*

---

7. Team Evaluation Template (Post-Ministry)

"Let us examine our ways and test them..." — Lamentations 3:40

Area	**Reflection Questions**	**Rating (1–5)**	**Comments**
Spiritual Preparedness	Did we pray, fast, and seek God as a team?		
Unity & Honor	Did we work together with		

Area	Reflection Questions	Rating (1–5)	Comments
	love and respect?		
Musical Execution	Were transitions smooth, was the team in sync?		
Congregational Engagement	Did we invite people into worship or just perform?		
Posture of Heart	Were we focused on God more than ourselves?		

Use this for personal AND team-wide feedback sessions.

---

8. Leadership Development Tracker

"You also must teach others..." —2 Timothy 2:2

Team Member	Current Role	Growth Area	Development Plan	Mentor Assigned
John	Background vocals	Lead with confidence	Co-lead 2 songs per month	Sarah
Anita	Sound operator	Spiritual depth	Join devotionals monthly	Pastor Lee

Update quarterly to track growth and plan handovers.

---

9. Worship Internship / Apprenticeship Plan

"Train up a child in the way he should go..."
Proverbs 22:6

Phase	Description	Duration	Outcome
Observe	Attend rehearsals/services	1 month	Understand team culture
Assist	Help with tech, setup, or simple parts	1–2 months	Serve behind-the-scenes
Participate	Join main worship as backup	2–3 months	Gain platform confidence
Lead	Lead set or devotion	1–2 months	Grow in leadership & self-evaluation
Multiply	Mentor new apprentice	Ongoing	Sustain multiplication

Assign each intern a mentor and check in monthly.

---

10. Worship Ministry Annual Calendar Template

Month	**Focus Area**	**Event or Activity**	**Purpose**
January	Refocus	Vision Casting & Prayer Night	Reset spiritual direction
March	Growth	Skill Development Workshop	Equip in new areas
May	Refresh	Worship Night	Minister to the church
July	Evaluate	Mid-Year Review	Identify growth and gaps
September	Multiply	Mentoring Launch	Train new leaders
November	Celebrate	Volunteer Appreciation Dinner	Honor and strengthen the team

Month	Focus Area	Event or Activity	Purpose
December	Rest	Team Sabbath Month	No new recruits or major events

Adapt based on local church rhythms.

Final Word to Worship Leaders

This toolkit is not just a resource—it's a framework for fruitfulness. Use it flexibly, faithfully, and prayerfully. And remember:

"You are not just building a team—you are building people.

You are not just shaping sound—you are shaping lives.

And you are not just leading songs—you are leading souls into the sanctuary of the Most High."

Appendix & Bonus Materials

"Let all things be done decently and in order." —1 Corinthians 14:40 (NKJV)
This appendix provides practical tools and ready-to-use templates that reinforce the key principles of the book. These resources help translate theory into action, ensuring the worship team is spiritually grounded, organizationally strong, and relationally healthy.

---

1. Sample Worship Team Handbook
"Write the vision and make it plain…" —Habakkuk 2:2
Purpose:
To clearly communicate the expectations, values, and structure of the worship ministry.
[Worship Ministry Handbook – Sample Template]
I. Vision & Mission
Vision Statement:
To lead our congregation into the presence of God through Spirit-filled, Scripture-rooted worship that glorifies Jesus Christ and transforms lives.
Mission Statement:
To build and disciple a worship team that ministers with humility, unity, and excellence, modeling a life of daily worship.

II. Our Core Values (with Scriptures)

Value	Description	Scripture
Christ-Centered	Jesus is the focus of every set, decision, and attitude	Colossians 1:18

Value	Description	Scripture
Servant Hearted	We lead by serving the Lord and others	Matthew 20:26–28
Humble Excellence	We offer our best without striving for spotlight	Colossians 3:23
Unity in Diversity	We celebrate our different gifts, united in purpose	1 Corinthians 12:12–27
Integrity	Our private lives must reflect what we lead publicly	Psalm 24:3–4

III. Team Expectations

- ✓ Be punctual for all rehearsals and services
- ✓ Come prepared with your parts practiced
- ✓ Prioritize spiritual preparation: prayer and devotion
- ✓ Maintain communication on scheduling and availability
- ✓ Attend at least one monthly team development meeting
- ✓ Resolve conflict biblically (Matthew 18:15–17)
- ✓ Submit to leadership and team guidelines
- ✓ Dress modestly and appropriately

IV. Team Structure

Role	Description
Worship Leader	Oversees the team spiritually, musically, and relationally
Band Leader	Coordinates instrumentalists and arrangements
Vocal Leader	Supports vocalists and harmonies

Role	Description
Sound/Tech Lead	Manages sound, media, and tech support
Mentor	Assigned to new team members for onboarding

V. Rehearsals and Services

- ✓ Weekly rehearsal: [Day, Time, Location]
- ✓ Call time for Sunday: [e.g., 8:00 AM sharp]
- ✓ Pre-service prayer is mandatory
- ✓ Services begin with readiness of **heart** and skill

VI. Leave of Absence / Rotation Policy

- ✓ Team members may request a sabbatical (1–3 months) for personal/spiritual reasons
- ✓ Absence beyond 3 weeks must be communicated in advance
- ✓ Monthly rotation schedules are confirmed 2 weeks ahead

VII. Team Covenant (Example)

- ✓ See Leader's Toolkit for full covenant template.

---

2. Scripture-Based Team Devotionals (8 Weeks)

"Let the word of Christ dwell in you richly…" — Colossians 3:16

Week 1: *The Heart of Worship*

Scripture: John 4:23–24

Reflection: True worship is not about location, genre, or style—it's about spirit and truth.
Question: What distracts me from worshipping in spirit and truth?

Week 2: *Called to Serve, Not Shine*
Scripture: Matthew 20:26–28
Reflection: Leadership in the Kingdom looks like serving others.
Action Step: Find one unseen way to serve this week.

Week 3: *Preparing the Altar*
Scripture: Romans 12:1
Reflection: Worship begins before Sunday—it's offering our lives daily.
Question: What area of my life needs surrender this week?

Week 4: *Guarding Unity*
Scripture: Ephesians 4:1–3
Reflection: Unity is worth fighting for—it creates a dwelling place for God.
Prayer Focus: Pray for every team member by name.

Week 5: *The Power of Praise*
Scripture: 2 Chronicles 20:21–22
Reflection: Praise precedes victory. Worship is spiritual warfare.
Group Activity: Share testimonies where worship brought breakthrough.

Week 6: *When Excellence Honors God*
Scripture: Psalm 33:3
Reflection: Skill and creativity reflect God's excellence—but they serve His glory.
Challenge: Practice your parts this week as an offering to God.

Week 7: *The Joy of His Presence*
Scripture: Psalm 16:11
Reflection: Joy is the fruit of God's presence, not performance.
Action: Choose joy in preparation, even in stressful moments.

Week 8: *Passing the Torch*
Scripture: 2 Timothy 2:2
Reflection: We are building legacy by discipling others.
Next Step: Identify someone you can encourage or mentor.

---

3. Worship Team Health Self-Assessment Tool

"Let us test and examine our ways..." Lamentations 3:40

Each member should rate the following areas from 1 (Rarely) to 5 (Consistently).
This is for personal growth, not criticism.

Area	Score	Reflection Question
I regularly spend personal time in prayer and Scripture		Am I worshipping privately before leading publicly?
I arrive on time, prepared musically and spiritually		Do I value team time as sacred?
I encourage and honor others on the team		Am I building others up in love?
I follow team communication and scheduling systems		Am I dependable and committed?

Area	Score	Reflection Question
I worship freely and lead authentically		Do I worship from my heart or perform out of habit?
I resolve conflict biblically		Am I guarding team unity?
I receive feedback with humility		Do I welcome correction and growth?
I pray for the congregation I serve		Am I spiritually interceding for our worship impact?

Total Score: ____ / 40
Areas to Grow:

____

Next Step/Prayer Point:

____

---

4. Worship Team Retreat Planning Guide
"Come aside... and rest a while." —Mark 6:31
A yearly or half-yearly retreat helps refuel the team spiritually, relationally, and creatively.
Retreat Objectives:

- ✓ Deepen team unity through shared experience
- ✓ Refocus on worship ministry's true purpose
- ✓ Train and inspire growth in both spirit and skill
- ✓ Provide rest, laughter, and renewal

Retreat Agenda (2-Day Format Example)
Day 1: Refresh & Refocus

- ✓ Morning Devotion: *"Come Back to the Heart of Worship"* (Psalm 95:1–7)

- ✓ Team-building activity: Worship-themed scavenger hunt
- ✓ Session 1: "The Spiritual Identity of a Worship Leader"
- ✓ Campfire Worship Night: Unplugged songs and testimony sharing

Day 2: Rebuild & Recharge

- ✓ Morning Prayer Walk / Soaking Worship
- ✓ Session 2: "Unity in Diversity" – Role-based breakout groups
- ✓ Creative Workshop: Songwriting, harmony building, or audio training
- ✓ Final Circle: Speak words of affirmation over each other
- ✓ Closing Communion & Commissioning Prayer

Retreat Essentials Checklist

- ✓ Venue booked with lodging & meals
- ✓ Worship equipment / portable sound
- ✓ Bibles, journals, pens
- ✓ Team devotional guide printed
- ✓ First-aid kit and emergency contact list
- ✓ Small budget for gifts/souvenirs or team shirts

Bonus Ideas:

- ✓ Invite a guest worship pastor or mentor for one session
- ✓ Provide 30 minutes of silence/solitude for reflection
- ✓ Create a “Worship Wall” where people write what worship means to them

---

Final Encouragement:

"They ministered to the Lord and fasted..." —Acts 13:2

Worship teams don't just prepare songs—they prepare themselves as living sacrifices. These tools are meant to help you build teams that are not just musically gifted, but spiritually grounded, relationally strong, and Kingdom-minded.

Build not just for the stage. Build for the sanctuary of God's presence.

About the Author
'GERARD ASSEY'

Gerard Assey is a Graduate in Economics, a PGD in Management (HRD) and holds a Doctorate in Leadership. Gerard holds several International Qualifications in Sales, Debt Collection, Training & Teaching, and is a 'Fellow' of the prestigious 'Institute of Sales & Marketing Management'-UK, a Certified NLP Practitioner, a 'Certified Trainer', an 'Accredited Management Teacher-Behavioral Sciences', a 'Certified Competency Facilitator', a 'Certified Management Consultant'- (the International credentials of a professional management consultant, awarded in accordance with global standards of the ICMCI); and a Certification from the University of Michigan in 'Successful Negotiation: Essential Strategies and Skills'

He is also a Member of the 'National Association of Sales Professionals' backed with several years experience in varied industries, both in India and Overseas. He also holds an 'Etiquette Consultant' Certification from the USA (by Sue Fox, Author of Best Seller: 'Business Etiquette for Dummies'. She has trained some of the top celebrities' world over). He was also a recipient of a scholarship for extensive training in Japan on 'Corporate Management for India'.

Gerard Assey is 'Founder & Chief Corporate Trainer' of the Group: '**Citius, Altius, Fortius Unlimited**'- an organization that **celebrated 20 years of Glorious Service** in 2021, focusing on 3 Core Competencies:

People. Performance. Profit; in functional areas of Sales & Marketing, HR & Organizational Development, covering Recruitment, Training & Consultancy!

Having managed organizations with large Sales Forces in India & Overseas, his specialization cover extensive areas of Sales Training (All levels - Presentation, Negotiation, Key/ Strategic Accounts Management & Managerial Skills for all sectors), Bid Proposal/ Capture Planning/ Management Trainings, Retail Sales, Customer Service & Customer Retention Programs, Training for Prevention & Collection of Debt, Self & Personal Development Programs (Time Management, Teamwork & Team Building, Business Etiquette & Personal Grooming, Leadership & Managerial Skills, People Management Skills, Train-the-Trainer etc), including preparation of Custom-designed Business Manuals for Internal (HR, Induction, and Sales etc) & External use (Instruction, User Manuals).

Gerard has successfully conducted over 6460 Trainings & Workshops (as of June '25) all across India, Middle East, Africa, Europe & S.E. Asia. Besides public programs conducted regularly, both in India & Overseas, he has some of the top names as clients whom he services from Single Owners to large Public & Government undertakings, covering all sectors, for their in-house needs.

His website: www.CollectionSkills.com is the only one in this part of the world to be featured in the 'Collections & Credit Risk Magazine-USA' under 'Who's Who in Training' and ranks TOP, along with other websites listed below on most search engines.

Gerard is author of 199 books already (July 2025), all the books being available on all online platforms and outlets as E-books and Paperbacks

A few of our business related books:

1. Bite-sized Bits on Commonsense Management
2. Heart to Heart on Life's Principles'
3. How to become a Successful Manager
4. The Sales Professionals' Master Workbook of S.Y.S.T.E.M.S
5. The Professional Business Email Etiquette Handbook & Guide
6. The Professional Business Video-Conferencing Etiquette Handbook & Guide
7. Professional Presentation Skills
8. Exceptional Customer Service
9. Professional Tele-Marketing Skills
10. Professional Debt Collection Skills
11. The G.R.E.A.T. Sales & Service Workbook
12. Sales Training Advantage for Results (*The Ultimate Sales Training Manual to enable you stand out as a S.T.A.R.*)
13. CEO Daily Planner & Organizer
14. The Sales Professionals' Master Daily Planner
15. The Professional Debt Collector's Master Daily Planner
16. My Daily Planner & Organizer
17. MY EMERGENCY INFORMATION RECORD (Family Emergency & Peace of Mind Planner)
18. The Ultimate Therapist & Counselors Planner and Organizer
19. Building an Ethical Workplace
20. Managing Relationships at Work
21. Managing Business Meetings Effectively
22. Effective Delegation Skills
23. Goal Setting for Success
24. B2B Selling by Email
25. Professional Business Etiquette & Grooming
26. Dining Etiquette & Table Manners
27. Effective Networking Skills
28. Grooming, Etiquette & Manners for Teens, Young Adults & Future Leaders
29. Inter-Personal Skills
30. Get Ready, Get Hired!
31. Selling in a Recession
32. Effective Receivables Management in an Economic Downturn!
33. Real Estate & Property Sales Training
34. Credit Sales & Accounts Receivable Management
35. Selling Skills for Real Estate & Property Advisors

36. Take G.R.E.A.T. C.A.R.E!
37. Spa, Salon & Health Club Selling Skills
38. Selling Travel, Holiday & MICE Services
39. Selling Skills for Spa's, Salons & Health Clubs
40. Retailing in Salons & Spas
41. Selling Holiday, Vacation, Tours & Packages
42. The Power of Sales Referrals
43. Selling Luxury
44. Technical Selling Skills
45. Financial Advisors Sales Training
46. Dealing with Burnout at Work Monopolize Your Markets
47. Selling to Affluent Customers
48. Growing up with Grace
49. Financial Selling Skills
50. *The Effective Manager's Guide: Key Skills to Thrive*
51. From Aspiring to Inspiring: A Guide for New Managers on the Rise
52. The Power of Focus
53. Selling with Integrity: Sell Like Jesus The Perfect Role Model!
54. 31 Habits of Champions: Your 31-Day Journey to Greatness
55. Rejecting Grasshopper Talk: From Grasshopper to Giant-Killer-*Defeating Giants Daily!*
56. Navigate the AI-Powered Future of Bid & Proposals: Up-Skill to Stay Relevant with Alternative Career Paths & Opportunities
57. Hiring Sales Winners
58. Present with Impact
59. Success Unlocked: *Breaking Free from Habits that Hold You Back*
60. Complaints to Cheers, Feedback to Gold: Mastering Complaints Management
61. Thriving Together: *Cultivating Diversity, Equity, and Inclusion*
62. Coaching Skills for Sales Managers
63. Soaring to Success in Business & Leadership: Swifter, Higher, Stronger!
64. From Classroom to Podium: A Student's Guide to Powerful Public Speaking & Presentation Skills
65. Developing Self-Discipline
66. The CEO's 31-Day Power Plan: Unlocking Success through Essential Traits
67. Credibility Matters

68. A Winning Attitude
69. Bid & Proposal Management Using AI
70. Sales Forecasting: A Practical & Proven Guide to Strategic Sales Forecasting
71. Elevate & Energize: *50 Dynamic & Fun Activities for Peak Workplace Morale*
72. 'Sales SOS! Sales on Fire! *30 Days to Conquer Chaos & the Nightmares of Success!'*
73. Mastering Sales Managerial Skills: *Building High-Performing Teams & Driving Exceptional Results*
74. Eagle-Eyed Leadership: Unleashing the Power of 31 Lessons from Eagles
75. The Ultimate Employee Training Guide: *Training Today, Leading Tomorrow*
76. Being More Accountable at Work
77. Creating a Culture of Continuous Improvement
78. Effective Questioning & Listening Skills
79. The Power of Value Selling
80. The Growth Mindset
81. Mastering Professional Help Desk Skills
82. The Power to Lead with Empathy
83. Being Prepared: The Key to Unlocking Success
84. Youthful Spark-Youth Energizers, Activities and Games-Igniting the Fun in Youth
85. Ignite your Motivation for Success
86. Elevate Your Executive Presence: *Your Roadmap to Executive Excellence*
87. Smart Decisions: *Mastering Problem Solving with Strategic Solutions for Business Success*
88. Strategic Planning: *Developing and Implementing Strategic Plans to Achieve Long-Term Business Goals*
89. The Power of Stay Interviews
90. Developing G.R.I.T.
91. Adaptability
92. Diagnosis- *A Key Skill for Leadership*
93. The Burnout-Proof Salesperson: *The Master Guide to Preventing Stress & Burnout*- Strategies for Thriving in Sales
94. Learning from Failure: *Keys to Success*
95. Customer Success Management
96. Overcoming the Killers of Motivation
97. The C-Suite Code: *Mastering Skills for Executive Excellence'*
98. Dealing with Difficult Customers

99. Unlocking Your Potential: Mastering the Top 20 Life Skills for a Brighter Future
100. Nurturing Tomorrow's Leaders: *Essential Soft Skills Every Child Must Learn*
101. Lively & Fun Party Games for Seniors & Elders
102. Role Playing for Sales Champions: From Practice to Performance
103. Fun and Exciting Party Games for Kids
104. Case Studies for Sales
105. Role-Playing for Unbeatable Customer Service
106. Case Studies in Customer Service
107. Case Studies in Winning Negotiations
108. Case Studies in Management & Leadership
109. Case Studies in Human Resources & Talent Management
110. CEO Success Blueprint: The Essential Toolkit for CEOs and C-Level Executives
111. The Salesperson's Self-Coaching Guide: *Master Your Own Self-Coaching Plan for Success*
112. Overcoming Procrastination: *Your Ultimate Guide to Stop Delaying and Start Living Your Best Life*
113. When True Colors Are Exposed: *The Journey to Unmasking Humanity*
114. Life-Changing Habits for Teens: Teen Success Blueprint for a Bright Future
115. Workplace Stress-Free: *Proven Strategies to Thrive at Work and Beyond*
116. Objection Overruled: *The Ultimate Guide to Turning 'No' into 'Yes'*
117. Building Strong Teams: *A Comprehensive Guide to Team Building*
118. Ethical & Moral Leadership in Business: *Eliminating Unethical Practices & Building a Culture of Trust & Integrity*
119. Rising Strong: Building Positive: High Self-Esteem for a Fulfilling Life-*A Practical Guide for Students, Employees, Leaders & Entrepreneurs*

From the Ministry side, Gerard graduated in the very first batch of Charis Bible College-India & had for over 9 years served as a Part-time Faculty at Charis Bible College-Chennai (Andrew Wommack Ministries-Colorado, USA). He also holds a Diploma in Worship (a subject closest to his heart) from the JSOW and is also a graduate of the Advanced Mentorship Program (AMP) and the Circle Of

Ministerial Engagement (C.O.M.E.) of Prophet Jerome Fernando and a Spiritual Son of the Esteemed Prophet. An accomplished author of several Secular & Christian Books, Gerard has been on the board of a few international organizations and boasts of being the SON of the MOST HIGH GOD: An ordinary guy following an extraordinary GOD!

...And some of his most recent Christian Books being:

1. A Bouquet of Praises for My KING
2. Christian Jokes for the Serious Religious' Folks!
3. Jesus Healed You!
4. Praise24Ever! (also in Tamil version)
5. The 5G Network of GOD
6. Building Faith over F.E.A.R- FACE EVERYTHING AND RISE with JESUS
7. Hebrew and Greek Praise and Worship Words
8. Godly Mothers' and Grandmothers' Bible Story time for Kids!
9. Miracles of Jesus in Pictures
10. Raise your Praise all 365 Days
11. Thanking GOD with an Attitude of Gratitude
12. Meditating on the Attributes of GOD
13. Puppet Scripts
14. Alcohol Ruins, JESUS Reforms, Renews & Restores!
15. Habakkuk 2:2 Christian Daily Journal, Planner & Organizer
16. ABC of GOD's Word for Handwriting Practice
17. Daily Bible Verse Handwriting Practice (Building Godly Character & Faith through Cursive Handwriting Practice!)
18. Guiding Light: Fun & Faith-Building Bible Activities for Children
19. Rejecting Grasshopper Talk: From Grasshopper to Giant-Killer-*Defeating Giants Daily!*
20. Teen Titans of Faith: *Building Courage, Determination & Christ-like-Esteem*
21. I AM Empowered: *Unleashing Divine Power with Positive Declarations*
22. Be A Solution Provider-*From Passion to Purpose*: *A Biblical Guide to Being the Answer to the World!*
23. Miracles of JESUS
24. Parables of Jesus for a Meaningful Life!
25. A Grateful Heart: Importance of Sharing Testimonies of GOD's Grace
26. Melodies of Worship to JESUS: 31 Songs of Praise & Worship From My Heart to HIS!
27. I AM SO BLESSED!
28. My Daily Cup of Energizer

29. 31 Leadership Lessons *from* Jesus- *The Supreme Leader*
30. Peace Amidst Storms: A Biblical Guide to Conquering S.T.R.E.S.S.
31. Rise Above: 20 Biblical Eagle Lessons for Life's Triumphs
32. Godly Goal Setting: *The FAITHFUL Blueprint for a Purpose-Driven Life*
33. The Profound Attributes of our Mighty GOD: Understanding the 10S's of the Almighty
34. Worship Now, Worship Forever: *A Journey from Earthly Praise to Eternal Glory*
35. Unceasing Praise & Worship: *365 Days to Worship the King*
36. The ROAR Within: *Living with Purpose and Authority through the Power of the Holy Spirit*
37. From Potential to Purpose: Unlocking and Multiplying Your Talents & Gifts for Kingdom Impact
38. Songs from the Heart: *Worshipping GOD in Your Own Tune & Melody*
39. Awakening Praise & Worship: Hebrew & Greek Words to Raise Your Praise
40. Sing a NEW Song to the LORD Everyday: *Daily Devotions of Praise & Worship to Lift Your Heart & Glorify HIS Name*
41. *The* A.R.O.M.A. of True Worship: *Creating Worship That Delights God*
42. Becoming A Kingdom Champion: *Embracing God's Call for a Life of Purpose & Victory*
43. The Busy Businessman's Daily Devotional: 366 Crisp Truths to Start Your Day Strong
44. The Teacher's Heart: *Daily Devotions for Educators*
45. Anchored! *A 31-Day Devotional for Students Facing Life's Challenges*
46. Suddenly! Unlocking Unorthodox Breakthroughs through Unusual Worship
47. Overcoming Adversity: *Lessons from the Bible for Modern Challenges*
48. LORD, Don't do it without me
49. Kingdom Leadership: *Biblical Principles for Modern Leaders*
50. Heartprints of God- *Growing God's Way:* Daily Devotions for Kids to Shine Bright
51. Send Judah First: Let your Praises Go up First to See the Mighty Move of GOD
52. DIVINE MOMENTS: *Recognizing, Embracing, Preparing, and Walking into Life-Changing Encounters with God*
53. Be a Builder in the Kingdom: *The C.E.M.E.N.T. Guide*

to Creating a Lasting Legacy

54. Unshakable: *Pillars of Godly Womanhood* (Pillars of Faith That Changed History)
55. Lead Like a Shepherd: *14 Essential Traits for Pastoral Excellence*
56. The Worship Leader's Arsenal: *Powerful Exhortations to Ignite Thanksgiving, Praise & Worship*
57. Women of UnShakable Faith: *31-Day Devotional for Strength, Purpose & Influence*
58. Called to Teach: *A Complete 10-Week Training Guide for Impactful VBS Teachers*
59. Strumming for the KING: Cowboy Songs of Faith & Fire
60. The Ultimate Youth Camp Playbook: *50 Bible-Centered Indoor Games to Engage, Equip, and Empower Teens*
61. Glad in HIS Presence: *David's Revelation of GOD's Love & Mercy*
62. The Spirit Behind the Sound: *52 Devotionals for Worship Teams*
63. THE COWBOY'S COMPASS: *Riding the Trail of Faith with Grit & Grace*
64. Worship as My Weapon: *Living Victoriously through the Power of Praise*
65. A Worshipper Always Wins*: Living a Life of Victorious Worship*
66. Worship That Leads to the Throne: *Practical Strategies for Worship Leaders to Inspire Their Team & Usher People into God's Presence*
67. Worship as Warfare: *Conquering through the Sound of Surrender*
68. Watchmen on the Walls: *A 31-Day Devotional for Worship Teams*
69. KINGDOM BUSINESS: *52 Biblical Principles for GODLY Leadership & Wise Decisions*
70. From Evening to Morning: *Rediscovering GOD's Sacred Hours*
71. Waves of Glory: *Worship through Dance, Flags, Staff & Sound*
72. WORSHIP TEAM BUILDER: *Guiding Your Team from Formation to Fruitfulness*

Besides regularly contributing to business & trade journals, including international ones such as the 'Creative Training Techniques' and the 'Sales News' of the U.S.A, He is also a member of several prestigious bodies & trade associations, having participated in many Conferences & Workshops in India & Overseas.

Prior to his last assignment of leading & managing a large MNC as head, Gerard had a 3-year stint in the Middle East as a Consultant with a leading British Consultancy Firm.

As the past 'Official Country Representative' for the International Business Award- 'THE STEVIES'-(the business world's own Oscar) for about 4 years- he ensured a few Indian companies that qualify for the same every year!

Gerard can be contacted at:

Email: training@Sales-Training.in,training@CollectionSkills.com
Websites:

www.Sales-Training.in
www.EtiquetteWorks.in
www.CollectionSkills.com
www.RetailSalesTraining.in
www.SalesTrainingIndia.com
www.ManualPreparation.com
www.TrainingWithPuppets.com
www.FirstContactAcademy.com
www.SalesAndMarketingRecruiter.com

www.ingramcontent.com/pod-product-compliance
Ingram Content Group UK Ltd.
Pitfield, Milton Keynes, MK11 3LW, UK
UKHW021342190726
13845UKWH00027B/674

9 788198 926272